the organic dog biscuit cookbook kit

from the

Bubba Rose

BISCUIT COMPANY

by

Jessica Disbrow Talley and Eric Talley

CIDER MILL
PRESS

BOOK
PUBLISHERS

KENNEBUNKPORT, MAINE

introduction

The Bubba Rose Biscuit Company was founded out of a desire to give dogs healthier treats and food. Tired of looking at long lists of preservatives and poor-quality ingredients in dog treats, and with an awareness about what we eat and where it comes from, we at Bubba Rose Biscuit Company became inspired to create treats from high-quality ingredients from foods we knew more about. We felt our dogs deserved it. Honestly, a bacon treat should actually contain bacon, not a laundry list of chemicals and artificial ingredients, right? We also thought everyone deserved to have their own recipes they could whip up at home for their good pups or on a special occasion – in fact, on any day. Dogs do know the difference with these homemade treats, we're certain of it. So try them out! There are lots of recipes in this book to choose from, and we guarantee your dog will be happy you put forth the effort.

13-Digit ISBN: 978-1-60433-054-0
10-Digit ISBN: 1-60433-054-6

This book may be ordered by mail from the publisher. Please include $2.75 for postage and handling. Please support your local bookseller first!

Books published by Cider Mill Press Book Publishers are available at special discounts for bulk purchases in the United States by corporations, institutions, and other organizations. For more information, please contact the publisher.

Cider Mill Press Book Publishers
"Where good books are ready for press"
12 Port Farm Road
Kennebunkport, Maine 04046
Visit us on the web!
www.cidermillpress.com

Design by Jessica Disbrow Talley
Printed in China

1 2 3 4 5 6 7 8 9 0
First Edition

ℰ It's Organic! ℨ

With people spending more time and energy to find out where their food comes from and how it is made, it's natural that their focus should turn, too, to wanting to know more about what they feed their pets. My husband Eric and I are both vegetarians, and we are careful about what we eat and where our food comes from, which led us to do the same for our dogs. After thoroughly researching our options, we decided to switch our dogs over to a raw diet made from organic produce and organically raised livestock. There is a lot to learn about this type of diet, but there is no reason your dog's treats can't be as healthy and natural as their food. (For more information on feeding raw, check out the Resources section in the back of the book.)

There are so many organically grown and manufactured products out there to choose from you should have no problem finding the best ingredients to make your treats out of. And if you do run into a problem finding an organic ingredient listed in any of these recipes, you can always swap it out for its non-organic counterpart (try to find a quality alternative, though). Your homemade treats aren't being certified, so do your best to make them with top-notch ingredients and your dogs will love you for it. We promise!

ξ Wheat, Corn & Soy Free ʒ

Every recipe in this book is free of wheat, corn and soy – the most common sources of food allergies in dogs. Avoiding these ingredients and still producing healthy, tasty treats is not hard – even in our 25 recipes! We know that dogs love treats so much they'll eat them regardless of the fact that their ingredients might make them itchy or not feel well afterwards. Using the recipes in this book, you can take pride in knowing your dogs (and any dog to whom you give these treats) will be happier and healthier.

ξ The Pantry List ʒ

This is a list of the dry ingredients used most frequently in the recipes in this book. Keeping them stocked and handy will make it easy for you to bake a fresh, quality treat for your dog any day of the week.

Organic oat flour
Organic brown rice flour
Organic oat bran
Organic garlic powder
Organic, all-natural peanut butter
    (or peanuts to grind your own; it's easy to do)
Organic honey
Organic applesauce (unsweetened)
Organic canned tuna and/or salmon

ℰ Stock the fridge (and freezer too) ℨ

Besides the dry ingredients listed above, there are a few items to have on hand in your refrigerator (or to keep frozen in the freezer) so you'll have them whenever you want to make treats.

Organic, shredded cheddar cheese
    (save time and buy pre-shredded)
Organic, grated parmesan cheese
    (save time and buy pre-grated)
Organic eggs
Organic bacon
    (this works especially well if you cook and drain it, then freeze it, so there is always some on hand when the mood strikes to bake dog treats)
Beef or chicken livers
    (these have a very short shelf life in the refrigerator, so buy them when you plan to bake, or freeze immediately for future use)
Organic chicken, turkey or beef
    (next time you are cooking any of these for your dinner, cook some without any seasonings or sauces and freeze it so you'll have the pre-cooked meat ready to use in your baking)

ℰ Substitutions ℨ

Baking dog biscuits is not rocket science. Things can easily be exchanged, added, or omitted, depending on what you have available or what your dog particularly likes. These recipes are all very easily adjustable. If you are making substitutions, just keep an eye on the dough consistency when mixing. If it's too dry, add more water. Too wet, add more flour. It's pretty simple. And keep an eye on the baking time. If they are browning faster than the time says, remove them from the oven. If they still look too light, add a few more minutes and keep an eye on them. Your dogs will love most things you make for them, so know they'll be happy even if you think you over- or under-cooked them a bit. Just be sure the meats you add are prepared according to the directions in the recipes.

ℰ Tools of the Trade ℨ

The following is a list of utensils and kitchen tools used in many of the recipes in this book; we highly recommend them. If you don't have them, there are alternatives to use, or you can mix and stir by hand. But from experience, we can say that the easier these are to make, the better. The more effort and mess that goes into these treats, the less likely you are going to want to make them again.

Rolling pin

So many of these recipes require you to roll out the dough before cutting it with either a cookie cutter, knife, pizza cutter or upside-down glass. You can cut the dough with many different items, but you really need the rolling pin to flatten the dough. They make nonstick rolling pins, which are a nice investment (you really don't want tuna in your next batch of cookies). But if you don't have one, to prevent the dough from sticking to your rolling pin (which happens since a lot of these doughs are a little sticky to work with) we recommend using a large plastic food-grade storage bag and placing it on top of your lightly floured dough - then roll away. It works like a charm.

Food processor

This truly is your kitchen wonder tool. You can use the grinding attachments to puree liver, make your own peanut butter, chop the cooked vegetables and meats down to fine pieces, etc... Besides, once you've finished the prep work, you switch to your dough attachment and let the machine mix the dough for you. You will still need to scrape the sides, but it cuts down on so much of the work you'll need to do. These machines are great; if you don't have one we wholeheartedly recommend them for your own personal use, as well. In our opinion, every kitchen should have one.

Aluminum foil

This makes clean-up a breeze. You don't want liver in the corners of your good cookie or jelly roll pans, do you? If you line your normal baking pans and sheets with a little aluminum foil first, all you have to do is peel it off and toss it when you're done, and your pans are ready for the next batch of oatmeal cookies you decide to whip up.

Cutting mat

We love the thin, plastic dishwasher-safe ones. Besides cutting and prepping your food on them, they are flexible, so you can curl them and slide all your ingredients directly into the mixing bowl.

Latex gloves

Some of the ingredients in the treats can be slightly unpleasant to work with. Who wants to mix a dough with tuna or liver in it and risk the smell permeating your hands when you work with it? Throw on a pair of disposable latex gloves (any supermarket carries them in their cleaning aisle) and work away. When you are done, drop them in the trash and keep your hands looking and smelling the way they should.

Cooking pans

This book contains a lot of recipes that use your standard cookie sheet or jelly roll pan. Some flat pan is probably necessary. There are also some recipes that require a muffin pan, mini muffin pan, mini loaf pans and square baking pans. If you don't have any of these, you can always skip that recipe and pick one for which you do have the pans - or substitute with something you have on hand. If you choose an alternate pan, know that you will need to keep an eye on the baking times, as they differ with the different thicknesses of the doughs or mixtures you are using.

ε Clean-Up Time Ʒ

As mentioned previously, covering your pans with aluminum foil is a great way to help save time during clean-up (and maintain the sweet integrity of your favorite cookie sheet). Also, using latex gloves will keep the smell off your hands. As stated in the recipes, when you are finished grinding up any of the less-than-pleasant-smelling ingredients – especially liver - rinse out your food processor immediately. These can become caked on very quickly and the dishwasher (or you and a sponge) will have a hard time getting them off. One lesson learned the hard way (we've had it happen, trust us, it's bad) and you'll always rinse those items immediately from now on.

ℰ Storage Tips ℈

Remember these recipes are all for homemade, preservative-free treats. With that in mind, they can't sit out the way processed dog treats that come in cardboard boxes can. We recommend storing any of these fresh-baked goodies in a plastic bag or container in the refrigerator. Even in there they will still mold, like your leftovers, so store only an amount you think you will use within a week. Any extras (since these recipes yield more than a week's worth of treats for most households) can be frozen to thaw out later (this works great) or given away as gifts to your friends, neighbors, or coworkers. Homemade dog biscuits are a great item to share. Spread the happiness!

ℰ Yields ℈

We tried to make these recipes as simple as possible and recommend using whatever you have on hand to form the shapes of the treats. That said, we can not state precisely how many treats each recipe will make. We also don't know your intended audience. If you have a Chihuahua, you'll obviously want to make smaller-sized treats (they'll also cook faster, so keep an eye on them). And if a Great Dane is your canine companion, make them larger (again, watch them, then they might need a little longer to cook). It's up to you, your dogs and what you have on hand. Most of the recipes are about the same size, so once you make one, you'll know how many extras you'll have the next time around.

ξ Soft or Crunchy? ℈

You know your dogs and their tastes or dietary needs. If you want the treats to be softer, cook them a little less or on a lower heat (definitely keep them in the refrigerator, too). If you want your treats to be a little harder, cook them longer at a lower heat. Or, when they are finished cooking, turn the oven off but leave them in there on the tray to cool for a few hours or overnight. Remember, this is all supposed to be an easy and fun thing to do for your beloved dogs. If they don't turn out perfectly, I bet you they won't mind one bit and will be so happy you made something special for them anyway.

ξ Resources ℈

There are thousands of websites of interest to dog owners these days, and the number of books on natural care continues to grow, too (how fortunate for us and our dogs!). We've been to quite a few of the sites and read lots of books, and this is our list of recommendations.

*Holistic Guide for a Healthy Dog (Howell Book House/
    John Wiley)*
*Dr. Pitcarin's New Complete Guide to Natural Health for
    Dogs and Cats (Rodale)*
*The Goldsteins' Wellness & Longevity Program:
    Natural Care for Dogs and Cats (TFH Publications)*
www.aspca.org
www.naturesvariety.com
www.vet.cornell.edu/library/freeresources.htm

THE PICK *OF THE* LITTER

A Collection of our Favorite Recipes

We compiled the top 25 recipes from our cookbook to create this best-of-the-best collection for you to utilize in making wonderful home-made treats for your dog, your best friend's dog and your dog's best friend. We hope you enjoy it! We know the dogs in your life certainly will.

Note: Choose to use organic ingredients in these recipes, as we do when we make them.

Pawlickin' Chicken   16
Grilled Cheese with Bacon   17
Biscuits and Gravy   18
Cheese, Please!   20
The Country Club   21
Liver & Bacon   22
Arroz con Pollo   24
Tuna Melt   25
Fish & Chips   26
Meat & Potatas   28
A Thanksgiving Prelude   29
Mambo Italiano   30
Snickerdoodle-poodle-poos   32
Plumpkins   33
The Classic   34
Banana B'oats   35
Energy Barks   36
Puppy Dog Eyes   37
Muddy Paws   38
Peanut Brittle   39
Under the Harvest Moon   40
Ohm These Are Good   42
Liver Alone   43
Jerky Turkey   44
Dragon Slayers   45

pawlickin' chicken

{ *These BBQ bites are the best!* }

1 c. oat flour

1 c. brown rice flour

1 c. ground chicken (cooked)

½ c. oat bran

2 Tbs. BBQ Sauce
   (select a sauce that does not contain onions or sugar)

1 egg

⅔ c. water

Preheat oven to 375°.

Combine all ingredients together and mix until a dough forms. Roll out on a lightly floured surface to ¼" thickness. Use a cookie cutter to cut into shapes. Line a cookie sheet with aluminum foil (for easy clean up), and place the cookies on the sheet (they can be rather close together as they don't grow much while cooking).

Bake 22-27 minutes. Transfer and let cool completely on a wire rack. Store the cookies in an airtight container in the refrigerator.

grilled cheese
with bacon

{ A wonderful addition to an all-time favorite }

1 c. oat flour

1 c. brown rice flour

$^1/_2$ c. shredded low-fat cheddar cheese

6 slices cooked bacon

1 egg

$^1/_2$ c. water

❋ ❋ ❋

Preheat oven to 350°. Cook bacon slices, then finely grind them in a food processor.

Combine all ingredients and mix thoroughly until a dough forms. Roll the dough out on a lightly floured surface to $^1/_4$" thickness. Use a cookie cutter to cut out shapes. Place on a cookie sheet lined with aluminum foil (easier clean up). Treats can be placed close together as they don't spread while cooking.

Bake for 20-25 minutes or until golden brown and cheese bubbles up. Remove from the oven and let cool completely on a wire rack. Store in an airtight container in the refrigerator.

biscuits
and gravy

Ɛ Start your day with a 'twang Ʒ

1 c. oat flour

1 c. brown rice flour

2 tsp. baking powder

1/4 c. extra-virgin olive oil

2 ground sweet Italian turkey sausages

1/2 c. chicken broth

✳ ✳ ✳

Preheat the oven to 450°. Place the sausages in a pot of water. Bring to a boil and cook for 20 minutes. Remove from heat and run under cold water until cool enough to handle. Remove the sausage casings and finely grind the sausage in a food processor.

Combine the cooked, ground sausage with all ingredients and mix thoroughly until a dough forms. Roll the dough out on a lightly floured surface to 1/4" thickness. Use a cookie cutter to cut into shapes. Place on a cookie sheet lined with aluminum foil (they can be rather close together as they don't grow much while cooking).

Bake 22-27 minutes or until the tops are golden brown. Remove from oven and let cool completely on a wire rack. Store in an airtight container in the refrigerator.

☞ Substitutions, Just do it!

The great thing about baking your own dog treats is that you can substitute many of the ingredients for items you have on hand or that you know your dog prefers. Since these flours are a little tricky to work with, I would avoid swapping those out as the recipe will require a good amount of adjusting with a different flour. But the main "flavor" ingredients can easily be switched around. For example, the above recipe calls for turkey and Swiss cheese. What if you have roast beef and provolone? Go ahead and use them instead. It's that easy throughout. If you want to swap tuna for salmon or chicken for turkey in a recipe, feel free. *Take note,* however: NEVER substitute an ingredient that may be toxic to dogs, such as onions, chocolate, raisins, macadamia nuts, and grapes.

cheese, please!

{ Loved by kids and dogs alike }

1 ½ c. oat flour

1 ½ c. brown rice flour

1 c. shredded low-fat cheddar cheese

½ c. grated parmesan cheese

1 egg

⅔ c. water

Preheat oven to 350°. Combine all ingredients and mix thoroughly until a dough forms. Roll the dough out on a lightly floured surface to ¼" thickness. Use a cookie cutter to cut out shapes. Place on an ungreased cookie sheet (they can be close together as they don't spread much while cooking).

Bake for 20-25 minutes or until golden brown. Remove from the oven and let cool completely on a wire rack. Store in an airtight container in the refrigerator.

the country club

℘ Three-par combo of apple, cheddar and bacon ℘

1 c. oat flour

1 c. brown rice flour

$^1/_2$ c. shredded low-fat cheddar cheese

$^1/_2$ c. applesause (unsweetened)

$^1/_2$ c. rolled oats (old-fashioned kind, not instant)

6 slices cooked bacon

1 egg

$^1/_3$ c. water

Preheat oven to 350°. Cook bacon then finely grind in a food processor.

Combine all ingredients and mix thoroughly until a dough forms. Roll the dough out on a lightly floured surface to $^1/_4$" thickness. Use a cookie cutter or a pizza cutter to cut out shapes. Place on a cookie sheet lined with aluminum foil (for easier clean up). Treats can be placed close together as they don't spread while cooking.
Bake for 20-25 minutes or until golden brown. Remove from the oven and let cool completely on a wire rack. Store in an airtight container in the refrigerator.

liver & bacon

Grandpa's favorite – but hold the onions

1 ½ c. oat flour

1 ½ c. brown rice flour

½ lb. raw beef or chicken livers

6 slices cooked bacon

1 c. oat bran

1 egg

½ c. water

Preheat oven to 375°. Puree livers in a food processor. Grind bacon into fine pieces in a food processor. Immediately clean the food processor afterwards - you definitely don't want either of these pulverized meats drying in your appliance. Cleaning this up if they do is not easy.

Combine all ingredients and mix thoroughly until a dough forms. Roll the dough out on a lightly floured surface to ¼" thickness. Use a cookie cutter to cut into shapes. Place on a cookie sheet lined with aluminum foil (keeps the icky ingredients off your cookie sheet and makes clean up a breeze). The treats can be placed close together as they don't spread much while cooking.

Bake for 22-27 minutes or until golden brown. Remove from the oven and let cool completely on a wire rack. Store in an airtight container in the refrigerator.

Note: For crispier treats, do not take them out of the oven to cool. Turn the oven off and let them sit in there overnight. Store in the refrigerator once removed.

 Liver – It's Time to Love It

Liver is an organ meat, and while all carnivores have been feasting on and benefiting from organ meats for as long as they've (we've) been roaming the planet, in the United States today, liver is much maligned as smelly and slimy. Add to that a reputation for being high in cholesterol, and it's no wonder it's not a popular choice for the family dinner table. But liver has long been an acceptable and desired ingredient in dog food and treats – and it's no wonder. Liver is loaded with vitamin A (retinol), which is good for your eyes, skin, and mucous membranes. It also contains vitamins E, D, and K, is packed with essential minerals, is a high-quality protein source, and is rich in omega-3 and omega-6 fatty acids. All these are great for your dog – and for you! One additional note: Because the liver is the detoxifying organ in the body, purchase meat that is as limited in its exposure to toxin-processing as possible, such as an organic cut.

arroz con pollo

❧ Just the right amount of heat – muy bueno! ❧

1 ½ c. oat flour

1 ½ c. brown rice flour

1 c. raw ground chicken

1 c. cooked brown rice

1 Tb. dried parsley

¼ tsp. garlic powder (or granulated garlic)

¼ tsp. cayenne pepper

1 egg

⅔ c. water (or chicken broth)

Preheat oven to 350°. Combine all ingredients together and mix thoroughly until a dough forms. Roll the dough out on a lightly floured surface to ¼" thickness. Use a cookie cutter and cut out the treats. Place on an ungreased cookie sheet (they can be rather close together as they don't spread while cooking).

Bake 20-25 minutes or until edges are golden brown. Remove from the oven and let cool completely on a wire rack. Store at room temperature in a loosely covered container.

tuna melt

ℰ Fries not included ℨ

1 c. oat flour

1 c. brown rice flour

$\frac{1}{2}$ c. oat bran

1 6-oz. can albacore tuna (in water)

$\frac{1}{2}$ c. shredded low-fat cheddar cheese

1 egg

$\frac{1}{2}$ c. water

Preheat oven to 350°. Pour entire contents of can of tuna (including all water and juices) into a food processor and finely grind.

Combine all ingredients and mix thoroughly until a dough forms. Add or decrease the water amount a little based on the amount of liquid in the can of tuna. Roll the dough out on a lightly floured surface to $\frac{1}{4}$" thickness. Use a cookie cutter to cut out shapes. Place on a cookie sheet lined with aluminum foil (for easier clean up and to keep tuna off your cookie sheets). Treats can be placed close together as they don't spread while cooking.

Bake for 20-25 minutes or until golden brown. Remove from the oven and let cool completely on a wire rack. Store in an airtight container in the refrigerator.

fish & chips

₹ The Irish Setter of snack foods ₹

1 ¼ c. oat flour

1 c. potato flour

½ c. oat bran

1 c. cooked cod (or another white fish)

¼ tsp. garlic powder (or granulated garlic)

1 egg

⅔ c. water

* * *

Preheat oven to 350°. Cook the cod thoroughly (use as little oil as possible). Finely grind it in a food processor.

Combine all ingredients and mix thoroughly until a dough forms. Roll the dough out on a lightly floured surface to ¼"thickness. Use a cookie cutter or a pizza cutter to cut out shapes. Place on a cookie sheet lined with aluminum foil (for easy clean up). Treats can be placed close together as they don't spread much while cooking.

Bake for 20-25 minutes or until golden brown. Remove from the oven and let cool completely on a wire rack. Store in an airtight container in the refrigerator.

 # Fish for Dogs

Everyone knows that fish is good for you, but why? And what about contaminants like mercury or other toxins? To answer the first question, fish is a rich source of important omega-3 fatty acids. These are the ones that support the optimal functioning of the heart, eyes, immune system, skeletal system, and skin and coat. Supplementing with omega-3-rich foods can benefit such conditions as allergies, arthritis, heart disease, and even cancer. Of course, it's important to find high-quality sources of fish so that its benefits aren't outweighed by what may be contaminating it – including mercury. That is why we recommend using wild-caught fish in our recipes.

meat & potatas

ξ *That's MEAT and POTATAS* Ʒ

1 c. oat flour

1 c. potato flour

$^1/_2$ c. oat bran

1 lb. lean ground beef (pre-cooked and drained)

1 tsp. dried parsley

$^1/_4$ tsp. garlic powder (or granulated garlic)

1 egg

$^2/_3$ c. water

Preheat oven to 375°. Cook and drain ground beef.

Combine all ingredients and mix thoroughly until a dough forms. Roll the dough out on a lightly floured surface to $^1/_4$" thickness. Use a cookie cutter to cut out shapes. Place on a cookie sheet lined with aluminum foil (for easy clean up and to keep beef off your favorite cookie sheet). Treats can be close together as they don't spread while cooking.

Bake for 20-25 minutes or until golden brown. Remove from the oven and let cool completely on a wire rack. Store in an airtight container in the refrigerator.

a thanksgiving prelude

{ An early start for the big day }

1 ½ c. oat flour

1 ½ c. brown rice flour

1 c. oat bran

1 c. mashed, cooked sweet potato

1 c. raw ground turkey

1 egg

½ c. water

✳ ✳ ✳

Preheat oven to 350°. Cook and mash the sweet potato.

Combine all ingredients and mix thoroughly until a dough forms. Roll the dough into 1" balls and place on a cookie sheet lined with aluminum foil (for easier clean up). Treats can be placed close together as they don't spread while cooking.

Bake for 22-27 minutes or until golden brown. Remove from the oven and let cool completely on a wire rack. Store in an airtight container in the refrigerator.

mambo italiano

⒠ Of course it's got rosemary! ⒠

1 ½ c. oat flour

1 ½ c. brown rice flour

1 6-oz. can tomato paste

½ c. fresh mozzarella, finely chopped

½ c. pureed roasted red peppers (optional)

½ c. grated parmesan cheese

1 tsp. dried rosemary

1 tsp. dried oregano

1 tsp. dried basil

¼ tsp. garlic powder (or granulated garlic)

1 egg

³/₄ c. water

Preheat oven to 350°. If using roasted red peppers, puree these in a food processor before doing anything else.

Combine all ingredients and mix thoroughly until a dough forms. Roll the dough out on a lightly floured surface to ¼"thickness. Use a cookie cutter to cut out shapes. Place on an ungreased cookie sheet (they can be close together as they don't spread while cooking).

Bake for 20-25 minutes or until golden brown. Remove from the oven and let cool completely on a wire rack. Store in an airtight container in the refrigerator.

☞ Rosemary for More Than Seasoning

Rosemary – like sage and thyme – is traditionally used to season foods, particularly roasted meats and vegetables. It is becoming more and more appreciated for its medicinal as well as gustatory benefits. Rosemary is a natural antibiotic and antiseptic. It also increases blood flow to the brain, aiding in memory and, when inhaled, rejuvenating the senses. It is a potent herb, and a little goes a long way – we could all use a little more often, though.

snickerdoodle-poodle-poos

{ What's in that again? }

1 ½ c. oat flour

1 ½ c. brown rice flour

2 tsp. cinnamon

1 egg

¼ c. honey

1 tsp. vanilla

⅔ c. water

* * *

Preheat oven to 375°. Combine all ingredients together and mix thoroughly in a large bowl. Spoon out mixture and roll into balls (about 1" in diameter). Place on an ungreased cookie sheet (they can be rather close together as they don't spread while cooking). Using a fork, press down the balls, flattening them and adding decorative lines in the tops.

Bake 18-22 minutes or until golden brown. Let cool completely on a wire rack. Store at room temperature in a loosely covered container.

plumpkins

Ɛ Pumpkin cookies dropped from heaven Ʒ

1 ¹/₂ c. oat flour

1 ¹/₂ c. brown rice flour

¹/₂ tsp. cinnamon

¹/₂ tsp. ground nutmeg

¹/₂ tsp. ground ginger

1 egg

3 Tb. applesauce (unsweetened)

³/₄ c. canned pumpkin (or fresh, pureed pumpkin)

¹/₂ c. water

Preheat oven to 350°. Combine all ingredients together and mix thoroughly. Spoon mixture out with a tablespoon and drop onto an ungreased cookie sheet. These cookies will not rise or flatten, so if you want a flatter cookie, press it down before baking.

Bake 18-22 minutes or until golden brown. Let cool completely on a wire rack. Store in an airtight container in the refrigerator.

the classic

*{ The keystone to any cookie jar –
the doggie version of the chocolate chip cookie }*

1 ½ c. oat flour
1 ½ c. brown rice flour
1 c. carob chips (can NOT be substituted with chocolate)
1 egg
1 tsp. vanilla
¾ c. water

Preheat oven to 350°. Combine all ingredients together and mix thoroughly. Roll into small balls (about 1" in diameter) and place on an ungreased cookie sheet (they can be rather close together as they don't spread while cooking). Press each one down with your hand to flatten the cookies.

Bake 18-22 minutes or until edges are golden brown. Let cool completely on a wire rack. Store at room temperature in a loosely covered container.

Note: Carob is a safe alternative to chocolate that does not contain the theobromine, caffeine, or other psychoactive properties of cocoa (which are potentially lethal in dogs). It is important to remember to NEVER give a dog chocolate.

banana b'oats

ξ Boatloads of oats and bananas ʒ

1 ½ c. oat flour

1 ½ c. brown rice flour

1 tsp. cinnamon

1 c. rolled oats (old-fashioned kind, not instant)

½ c. oat bran

1 egg

½ c. bananas (mashed & pureed)

½ c. water

✳ ✳ ✳

Preheat to 350°. Combine all ingredients together and mix thoroughly. Roll into small balls (about 1" in diameter) and place on an ungreased cookie sheet (they can be rather close together as they don't spread while cooking). Press each one down with your hand to flatten the cookies.

Bake 18-22 minutes or until edges are golden brown. Let cool completely on a wire rack. Store at room temperature in a loosely covered container.

energy barks

Powers your dog up for a whole day of digging

1 ¼ c. oat flour

1 ¼ c. brown rice flour

½ c. rolled oats (old-fashioned kind, not instant)

½ c. granola (can not contain raisins)

1 egg

¼ c. molasses (blackstrap or regular)

⅔ c. water

✳ ✳ ✳

Preheat oven to 350°. Combine all ingredients together and mix thoroughly. Roll into small balls (about 1" in diameter) and place on an ungreased cookie sheet (they can be rather close together as they don't spread while cooking). Press each one down with your hand to flatten the cookies.

Bake 18-22 minutes or until edges are golden brown. Let cool completely on a wire rack. Store at room temperature in a loosely covered container.

puppy dog eyes

Ɛ Nobody can resist these adorable carob puppy dog eyes! Ȝ

1 ½ c. oat flour

1 ½ c. brown rice flour

1 c. carob chips (can not be substituted with chocolate)

1 egg

½ c. peanut butter (unsalted)

⅔ c. water

Preheat to 350°. Combine flours, egg, peanut butter and water and mix thoroughly. Roll into small balls (about 1" in diameter) and place on an ungreased cookie sheet (they can be rather close together as they don't spread while cooking). Use your thumb to press an indent into the center of each cookie. Evenly sprinkle a few of the remaining carob chips into the center of each cookie (they should pool while cooking and look like a brown dot when cooled).

Bake 18-22 minutes or until edges are golden brown. Let cool completely on a wire rack. Store at room temperature in a loosely covered container.

muddy paws

ε The only acceptable kind to have in the house З

1 ½ c. oat flour

1 ½ c. brown rice flour

¼ c. carob powder (can not be substituted with chocolate)

½ c. carob chips (can not be substituted with chocolate)

1 egg

½ c. peanut butter (unsalted)

1 Tb. honey

⅔ c. water

Preheat oven to 350°. Combine all ingredients together and mix thoroughly. Roll into small balls (about 1" in diameter) and place on an ungreased cookie sheet (they can be rather close together as they don't spread while cooking). Press each one down with your hand to flatten the cookies.

Bake 18-22 minutes or until edges are golden brown. Let cool completely on a wire rack. Store at room temperature in a loosely covered container.

peanut brittle

It'll inspire you to break out the pinochle!

3 c. brown rice flour

1 tsp. cinnamon

1 egg

$^1/_2$ c. honey

$^1/_4$ c. molasses (blackstrap or regular)

$^1/_2$ c. peanut butter (unsalted)

$^1/_4$ c. safflower oil

1 c. finely chopped peanuts (unsalted)

Preheat oven to 325°. Combine all ingredients except the peanuts in a food processor until completely mixed. It should form a stiff dough. Press the dough into a jelly roll pan or cookie sheet with edges. Place plastic wrap or parchment paper over the pan and smooth down the mixture to $^1/_4$" thick. Remove and discard wrap or paper. Press the remaining chopped peanuts into the mixture. Use a knife to score the dough into individual sized portions.

Bake 30-40 minutes or until the edges are golden brown. Cool completely in the pan on a wire rack. Once cool, break apart using the scored lines. Store in a loosely covered container at room temperature.

under the harvest moon

ξ A cornucopia of earthly delights 3

1 c. oat flour

1 c. brown rice flour

$^{1}/_{2}$ c. rolled oats (old-fashioned kind, not instant)

$^{1}/_{2}$ c. hulled sunflower seeds (unsalted)

$^{1}/_{2}$ c. pureed carrots

$^{1}/_{2}$ c. cooked, pureed butternut squash

$^{1}/_{2}$ c. pureed broccoli

$^{1}/_{4}$ tsp. garlic powder (or granulated garlic)

1 egg

$^{1}/_{4}$ c. water

*These treats are high in fiber, low in fat,
meat-free, and low in protein.*

Preheat oven to 350°. Peel, dice and finely grind carrots in a food processor. Cook, dice and finely grind butternut squash in a food processor. Finely grind broccoli in a food processor.

Combine all ingredients together in a food processor (or mix by hand in a bowl) until a dough forms. Spoon mixture out with a tablespoon and drop onto an ungreased cookie sheet. These cookies will not rise or flatten, so if you want a flatter cookie, press it down before baking.

Bake 20-25 minutes. Remove from the oven and let cool completely on a wire rack. Store in an airtight container in the refrigerator.

 Pumpkin Anytime!

Pumpkin is a nutritious and delicious food whose benefits can be reaped by including it in recipes that go well beyond the traditional holiday pie – and your dog shouldn't be getting any of that pie, anyway! Pumpkin is high in potassium and beta carotene (a natural antioxidant) but low in calories, so when steamed and eaten in chunks or pureed, pumpkin is great for those watching their weight who want to enjoy a flavorful and filling veggie. A tablespoon or two of canned (or fresh) pumpkin added to their food will firm up your dog's stool if he has diarrhea, or help loosen it if he is constipated (it's true, it works both ways). It's a miracle food!

ohm my
these are good

{ Helps their bellies achieve a zen-like state }

1 c. oat flour

1 c. brown rice flour

1 c. canned pumpkin (or fresh pureed pumpkin)

1 tsp. cinnamon

1 egg

1/3 c. water

*These treats are high in fiber, low in fat,
meat-free and low in protein.*

Preheat oven to 350°. Combine all ingredients together and mix until a dough forms. Roll into small balls (about 1" in diameter) and place on an ungreased cookie sheet (they can be rather close together as they don't spread while cooking).

Bake 20-25 minutes. Remove from the oven and let cool completely on a wire rack. Store in an airtight container in the refrigerator.

liver alone

ℰ ... but not in exile ℈

1 ½ c. tapioca flour
  (or garbanzo bean flour or amaranth flour)

1 lb. beef livers (or chicken livers)

2 eggs

This treat is grain-free.

Preheat oven to 300°. Puree liver in a food processor. Immediately clean it afterwards, as liver makes an awful mess if left in there to dry.

Combine all ingredients together and mix thoroughly. Line a jelly roll pan with aluminum foil (it helps make clean up a breeze). Pour mixture into the pan.

Bake for 30 minutes. Cut into shapes using a cookie cutter. Remove from the oven and let cool completely on a wire rack. Store in an airtight container in the refrigerator.

Note: To make crunchier treats, put them back in the oven (after cutting them) for an additional 2 hours at 150°.

jerky turkey

*❧ One tough bird, but one
gentle-on-the-tummy treat ❦*

1 lb. raw ground turkey (or chicken)

1 Tb. extra-virgin olive oil

¼ tsp. garlic powder (or granulated garlic)

This treat is grain-free and low in fat.

Preheat oven to 200°. Combine all ingredients together in a food processor and puree the mixture. Line a jelly roll pan with aluminum foil (it makes clean up easier) and pour the mixture into it. Spread evenly.

Bake 2 hours with the oven door slightly ajar to allow the moisture to escape. Remove from oven, and using a pizza cutter or knife, cut into small individual-sized portions. Place pieces back in the oven, flipped over, and bake an additional 1-2 hours or until the treats are dry and leathery. Store in an airtight container in the refrigerator.

dragon slayers

ξ Helps to banish the foul beast that is bad breath! ʒ

1 c. oat flour

1 c. brown rice flour

3 Tbs. applesauce (unsweetened)

½ c. dried mint

½ c. dried parsley

1 egg

¾ c. water

This is a low-fat, meat-free treat.

Preheat oven to 350°. Combine all ingredients together and mix until a dough forms. Roll into small balls (about 1" in diameter) and place on an ungreased cookie sheet (they can be rather close together as they don't spread while cooking).

Bake 20-25 minutes. Remove from the oven and let cool completely on a wire rack. Store in an airtight container in the refrigerator.

ℰ *About Bubba Rose Biscuit Co.* ℨ

My husband Eric and I founded the Bubba Rose Biscuit Company in 2006 out of our desire to give our dogs healthier treats and food. Since the company's founding, we have been baking biscuits and making dogs happy from coast to coast – and even overseas.

Let us introduce the test group: We have the humans, Jessica and Eric Talley (co-founders of the company and co-authors of this book) - animal lovers and rescuers since day one. The list of pets we've cared for, prior to the pups, includes: guinea pigs, gerbils, sugar gliders, bunnies, a turtle, chameleons, a collared lizard, geckos, tree frogs, water frogs, fish, a snake, and a cat. There's no shortage of animal love and experience here.

And we have the pups: Bob (also called Bubba, Bobby Sue, Meat, and Biscuit), our beloved rescued Pit Bull. He's the sweetest, most affectionate 60-pound lap dog ever. Then there's Rose (also called Miss Rosetta [her racing name], Goose, Mama, and Greyhound), our precious Greyhound. She is the most delicate, intelligent, and gentle dog - and lazy as can be! And gone but not forgotten, we have Weeble (or Little Man, Monster and Stinky), he was our wacky little rescued Shih Tzu puppy. He was the happiest and most playful little guy. He has passed on since our first book, but he's always in our hearts.

That's the gang. And we have to get back to baking now – there are some hungry dogs waiting on us!

Visit us at ☞ www.bubbarose.com

ℰ About Cider Mill Press ℈

Good ideas ripen with time. From seed to harvest, Cider Mill Press strives to bring fine reading, information, and entertainment together between the covers of its creatively crafted books. Our Cider Mill bears fruit twice a year, publishing a new crop of titles each spring and fall.

CIDER MILL
PRESS

BOOK
PUBLISHERS

Where good books
are ready for press

Visit us on the web at:
www.cidermillpress.com

Or write to us at:
12 Port Farm Road
Kennebunkport, Maine 04046